looking at art

6

MYTH & RELIGION

Grolier Educational

SHERMAN TURNPIKE, DANBURY, CONNECTICUT 06816

Grolier Educational
Grolier Publishing Company, Inc.

Grolier Educational Staff
Joseph Tessitore, *Senior Vice President, Sales and Marketing*
Robert B. Hall, *Senior Vice President, Sales*
Beverly A. Balaz, *Vice President, Marketing*
A. Joseph Hollander, *Vice President and Publisher, School and Library Reference*
Molly Stratton, *Editor, School and Library Reference*

This edition first published 1996 by Grolier Educational, Danbury, Connecticut 06816.
Copyright © 1996 Marshall Cavendish Limited.

ISBN 0-7172-7595-7 (set)
ISBN 0-7172 7601-5 (volume)

Cataloging information can be obtained directly from Grolier Educational.

Marshall Cavendish Limited
Editorial staff
Series Consultant: Anthea Peppin,
Senior Education Officer, National Gallery, London
Series Editor: Tim Cooke
Editor: Sarah Halliwell
Senior Designer: Wayne Humphries
Picture Rights Coordinators: Vimu Patel, Sophie Mortimer
Text: Mark Ravenhill
Index: Susan Dawson
Printed in Malaysia

J. Ref
709
mgt

Contents

1: Early & Renaissance Art   *4*

The Venus de Milo   *6*

The Expulsion from Paradise • *Masaccio*   *8*

The Last Supper • *Leonardo da Vinci*   *10*

Hell • *Hieronymus Bosch*   *12*

The Crucifixion • *Matthias Grünewald*   *14*

2: The Seventeenth & Eighteenth Centuries   *16*

Medusa • *Michelangelo Merisi da Caravaggio*   *18*

The Deposition • *Peter Paul Rubens*   *20*

The Judgment of Paris • *Claude Lorrain*   *22*

3: The Nineteenth Century   *24*

Dido Building Carthage • *J.M.W. Turner*   *26*

Rouen Cathedral • *Claude Monet*   *28*

The Vision after the Sermon • *Paul Gauguin*   *30*

The Gates of Hell • *Auguste Rodin*   *32*

4: The Twentieth Century   *34*

Orpheus • *Odilon Redon*   *36*

White Crucifixion • *Marc Chagall*   *38*

Pasiphaë • *Jackson Pollock*   *40*

Pope Innocent X • *Francis Bacon*   *42*

GLOSSARY   *44*

INDEX   *45*

FURTHER READING   *48*

PICTURE CREDITS   *48*

Early & Renaissance Art

From earliest times art has been an effective way of telling religious stories to ordinary people. During the Renaissance paintings were also used to tell ancient myths from the classical times that artists admired.

From the 15th century onward, artists working in the city-states of Italy saw themselves as helping to create a "renaissance"—a rebirth of learning and art. They believed that the art of the ancient cultures of Greece and Rome was better than that of the civilizations that had come after. They divided history into three stages: the classical Greek and Roman period, which they admired; the "middle ages," which they believed to be an uncultured and barbaric period; and their own glorious era—the Renaissance.

Teaching the people

During the Middle Ages Europe's most powerful organization had been the Church, which paid for almost all the pictures painted. The most popular subjects were scenes from the Bible, especially the life of Jesus. But the Bible and the sermons given in church were in the ancient language of Latin, which ordinary people did not understand. So paintings became a way of teaching them about religion.

Although the Church remained very powerful, from the 14th century a new class began to emerge. This section of society was made up of families whose wealth came from trade and banking. Many such families lived in Italy. The people living in Italian cities wanted to create a culture to rival that

Three Graces: Roman sculpture
This ancient sculpture was preserved by layers of ash from the volcano that destroyed Pompeii in A.D. 79.

of the Greeks and Romans. They started to commission artists to paint the fantastic myths and legends of the ancient world.

A classical inspiration

Because little classical painting survived, these Renaissance artists were most influenced by ancient statues. When Botticelli painted *Primavera*, he first consulted the tutors of the young nobleman who would own the finished work. The picture would be used to teach the young man about classical myths. Can you see how Botticelli's

portrayal of the Three Graces—goddesses who personified grace, charm, and beauty—is like the statue of the sisters from ancient Pompeii?

While they were fascinated by the classical world, the people of the Renaissance were Christians, and so many paintings still showed Bible stories. Wealthy families paid for pictures and donated them to the Church or put them in their own private chapels.

During the Middle Ages figures in paintings had appeared flat, with little individuality. But in the Renaissance the study of anatomy—the way the human body works—and perspective, a technique for making things look three-dimensional, helped bring new realism to depictions of familiar biblical and mythological stories.

Primavera: Sandro Botticelli
The figure in the center is Venus, goddess of Love; Cupid hovers above her head. Can you spot Mercury, messenger of the gods?

The Venus de Milo

Greek statue, about 100 B.C.

For more than a thousand years southern Europe was dominated by classical civilization—first by the Greeks and then by the Romans. These cultures believed in clarity, balance, and moderation in both life and art.

Both the Greeks and the Romans believed that there were many gods. They thought that each god controlled a particular aspect of human life such as war, music, or love. The

Greeks called their goddess of love Aphrodite, after the Greek word for waves, because she was said to have come from the sea. Then, when the Romans became the most powerful nation in Europe, they adopted many of the Greek gods but gave them new names. In Roman myth Aphrodite became known as Venus.

In 1820 this statue of the goddess was rediscovered by accident on the Greek island of Melos and rescued from destruction in a kiln, where it would have been heated to make lime dust for cement. Experts think the statue was originally part of a group in which Venus would have been reaching out her arms to her little son Cupid, also a god of love.

The Greeks were not interested in showing individual men and women but wanted to create images of what they considered to be perfect beauty. Can you see how this statue's sculptor avoided giving the face a particular expression? He wanted to concentrate on the body and its movement instead. You can see the outline of Venus's knee beneath the thick drapery. Even though this statue is no longer whole, look how graceful and elegant it is. Many Renaissance artists looked on similar statues as ideals of beauty.

The Expulsion from Paradise

by Masaccio (about 1401–1428)

The Italian painter, whose first name was Thomas, was nicknamed "Masaccio," which means Clumsy Tom. Although he died when he was only 27, he was one of the most important and innovative painters of the 15th century.

Masaccio painted this fresco in the Brancacci Chapel, in the church of Santa Maria del Carmine in Florence. A fresco was a picture painted onto a

wall: the paint was applied to the plaster while it was still wet, and the plaster and paint dried together, fixing the picture.

The fresco shows Adam and Eve being thrown out of Paradise. The Bible tells how God banished Adam and Eve, the first man and woman, from the Garden of Eden because they disobeyed him by eating the fruit of the Tree of Knowledge.

In Masaccio's painting the angel guarding the gate of Eden expels Adam and Eve. Look closely at their faces: their reactions are intensely human. Adam covers his face in grief and shame, while Eve tries to hide her nakedness, her face contorted in a wail of agony. It is not just the couple's faces that express their terrible suffering: look how their bodies are tense and strained. The figures seem heavy and bulky, like statues. They are illuminated by a harsh white light.

Masaccio strips everything in the scene down to the absolute essentials in order to express a sense of raw emotion. Artists had painted this story many times before—but no one had captured the human tragedy of the scene in such a dramatic way.

The Last Supper

by Leonardo da Vinci (1452–1519)

At the Last Supper—the final meal that he shared with his followers—Jesus, the calm figure in the center, has just announced that one of the 12 men with him will betray him to his enemies. Look at the shock his words have created. Some of the diners look horrified, disbelieving, or angry, while others wonder who the traitor might be. Can you pick out Judas, the man who will betray Jesus for 30 pieces of silver?

Artists usually showed the disciples as a group with Judas set apart or at the other side of the table. But here Judas can be distinguished by his expression: he recoils from Jesus, his fist clenched and his face dark with guilt and anger. Look how the picture is organized. The 12 disciples fall into four groups of three, and each person gestures and whispers. What do you think they might be saying? No previous painting of the story had shown the disciples reacting in such a variety of different, very human, ways.

In 1497 the Italian Leonardo was asked to paint this wall painting in the dining room of a monastery. When the head of the monastery complained that the artist was taking too long to finish the picture, Leonardo threatened to paint Judas with the abbot's face. The complaints soon stopped.

Leonardo often experimented with different kinds of paint. Here he used

a mixture of tempera and oil. Unfortunately this experiment was not successful, but even though the colors have deteriorated, the action of the painting is still striking.

Can you imagine the reaction of the monks when they first saw this powerful image? Look how Leonardo has used perspective to create space. It looks almost as if this dramatic religious story is taking place in an extension of the monks' own dining room.

Hell

by Hieronymus Bosch (about 1450–1516)

Doesn't this seem a strange painting to stand above the altar in a Dutch church? In a nightmarish landscape of burning buildings, black water, and dry earth, a mass of naked men and women are being tormented by animal-like devils. In the center a weird figure—half man, half tree, with a body like a broken eggshell—looks out over the scene of violence and destruction. It is an unusual and original vision of Hell. Do you think it is frightening?

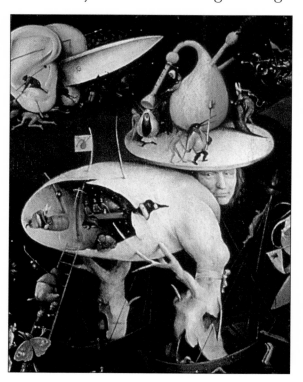

Each detail in this huge painting is a warning about a particular sin. Can you see the enormous ears pierced by a knife, for example? This represents eavesdropping, or listening to others' conversations. And the woman sitting under the huge stool looking into a mirror represents vanity.

This painting had a serious moral purpose—to warn people that if they did bad things they would go to Hell, where these punishments awaited them. But the painter Hieronymus Bosch also seems to enjoy creating this bizarre and hideous world.

Bosch was born far away from the center of the Italian Renaissance, in the Dutch town of Hertogenbosch. Although the town had no court or university as the Italian city-states did, there were many rich and powerful churches, and it was for these that Bosch produced his paintings.

This painting is part of a triptych—a series of three paintings hinged together—called *The Garden of Earthly Delights*. The first part of the painting shows Adam and Eve's life in Paradise, while the second, and biggest, picture shows men and women indulging in sins. This right-hand panel shows the terrible consequences of these sins. Would it encourage you to be good?

The Crucifixion

by Matthias Grünewald (about 1470–1528)

In Roman times criminals were punished by being crucified. They were nailed to a wooden cross by their hands and feet and left to die very slowly and painfully. In the Bible this is how Christ is put to death. But because it was believed that Jesus was the son of God, paintings of the Middle Ages did not show him suffering on the cross. Artists showed him as calm and serene, waiting to return to his father in Heaven. Later, Italian painters of the Renaissance, influenced by the Greek ideals of physical perfection, also avoided showing Christ's physical torment in their pictures of the Crucifixion.

The German painter Grünewald painted the Crucifixion at least four times—usually to decorate church altars—and he had a different way of approaching the subject from the Italians. He had a clear lesson to teach people. The Bible tells us that Christ was crucified because of the sins of humanity; Grünewald wanted to remind people that it was their own sins that caused Christ's suffering.

In the painting Mary, the mother of Jesus, stands to his left, and Saint John stands to his right. Look how weak Jesus' body looks; his muscles are twisted and strained. His pale, gray-looking skin is bleeding and cut, and his loincloth is torn and dirty. His face is contorted in pain beneath a cruel spiky crown of thorns.

Grünewald concentrates on the physical agony and horror of being crucified: Christ's suffering is as real as if he were any ordinary human being. Grünewald emphasizes Christ by making him much larger than Mary or John. Look how huge his hands and feet are compared to the pale hands that Mary clasps together.

The Seventeenth & Eighteenth Centuries

While Protestants did not believe in decorating churches, artists were employed by Catholic churches to produce elaborate and emotional works intended to dazzle the viewer and encourage their faith.

Early in the 16th century a religious movement began in the north of Europe which became known as the Reformation. Its originators—priests such as Martin Luther—thought that the Catholic Church was too interested in grand ceremony and wealth.

They declared their independence from the Pope, the head of the Catholic Church, and set up their own Protestant churches where they pursued simpler forms of worship. One of the things they rejected was the overdecoration of churches and so the tradition of religious painting declined in the new Protestant countries.

Images of faith

The Catholic Church responded to these changes by setting up its own Counter-Reformation to reassert its power. By the end of the 16th century the Catholic and Protestant countries had reached a stalemate.

As the confidence of the Catholic Church grew again, so did the splendor of the works of art it paid for. When the patron of the artist Bernini became pope in the middle of the 17th

The Ecstasy of Saint Theresa: Gianlorenzo Bernini
Bernini creates drama in this sculpture. Look how expressive Theresa's face is.

century, he commissioned Bernini to decorate a chapel and square in Rome. Bernini created a statue of Saint Theresa, a 16th-century Spanish nun who had a vision in which an angel from God pierced her heart with a burning golden arrow, filling her with both agony and great joy.

A masterpiece in marble

Look how Bernini shows the saint being carried toward heaven on a cloud as the angel approaches. Rays of sun stream about her, and her eyes are closed in ecstasy. The sculpture seems to hover in the air without any support. Light from a hidden window above bathes the statue, increasing its dramatic effect.

Some people did not like this kind of art. They thought it was too showy and theatrical. But the style—known as Baroque—soon established itself. Artists such as Rubens (*see page 21*) spread its popularity to the countries in northern Europe that were still Catholic.

A less mysterious world

The world was becoming a less mysterious place. In 1492 Columbus had sailed to America. Other Europeans made many voyages to trade or to claim territory in unknown lands. Scientists such as Galileo and Newton discovered simple laws that could help explain some of the great questions of nature and the universe.

Art reflected this diminishing sense of mystery. By the early 17th century the Italian artist Caravaggio (*see page 19*)

was using real men and women as models for his paintings. Although the subjects were still religious and mythic, his images captured ordinary people at dramatic moments.

Caravaggio's paintings influenced many artists, including Artemesia Gentileschi. In her dark and tense painting *Judith with Her Maidservant* she depicts two characters from the Old Testament as very real and powerful women committing a crime.

Judith with Her Maidservant:
Artemesia Gentileschi
Judith, a Jewish widow, seduced an enemy general and then murdered him.

Medusa

by Michelangelo Merisi da Caravaggio (1571–1610)

According to Greek legend, Medusa was one of three terrible sisters called the Gorgons. The Gorgons had fangs for teeth and snakes for hair. Whoever looked at them was instantly turned to stone.

In the myth, the hero Perseus had to kill Medusa in order to protect his mother from a god. To avoid the Gorgon's fatal glare, Perseus approached her by using his polished shield as a mirror so that he only had to look at

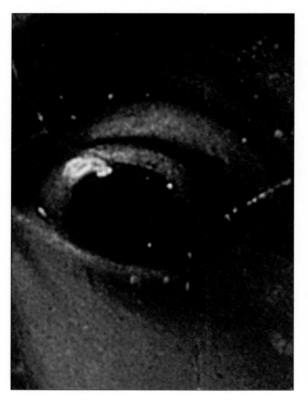

her reflection. In this way he was able to get close enough to cut off her head with his sword. Even after Medusa was dead, however, the head still kept its powers. A great goddess called Athena eventually attached it to the front of her own shield in order to defeat her enemies.

Caravaggio painted his image of Medusa on a round shield, in keeping with this ancient story. His painting shows the gory moment after Perseus has struck her head from her body. Look at the expression on Medusa's face. Artists traditionally painted figures from Greek legends according to the ideals of beauty they found in ancient Greek and Roman statues. But Caravaggio took a different approach: his evil Medusa looks all too human with her very real expression of terror and shock.

Caravaggio creates drama by using strong contrasts of light and shadow. He often painted in a dark studio, with only a single carefully placed lamp throwing shadows on the models that he used. Look how in this picture the light comes from the left, making the writhing snakes glisten and capturing the fear in Medusa's eyes. A dark shadow falls on the right-hand side of the shield.

The Deposition

by *Peter Paul Rubens (1577–1640)*

The Bible tells the story of Joseph of Arimathea, a rich follower of Jesus. Joseph was determined that, after Christ had been crucified, he should have a proper burial. Pontius Pilate, the Roman governor who had sentenced Jesus to death, agreed to this request. So, by night, Joseph and his friend Nicodemus lowered Jesus' body from the cross and wrapped him carefully in a sheet. This event was traditionally known as the descent from the cross, or the Deposition.

Rubens worked in the Netherlands most of his life, but he visited Italy and was influenced by the paintings that he saw there. Can you see how the strong contrast between light and dark in this picture shows the influence of Caravaggio *(see page 19)*? The lighting adds drama to a scene where everyone otherwise seems very still.

Think how upsetting and unpleasant a picture of this subject could be. But Rubens emphasizes the beauty of the scene. The wealth of Joseph and his friends is shown by the rich colors of their clothes. They are carefully grouped around the passive body of Christ, which stands out against the bright white cloth. Look how pale, limp, and heavy his body looks, in contrast with the strong muscular bodies of the men who gently let him down from the cross.

Did you notice at the foot of the ladder the crown of thorns and the nails that have already been taken out of Christ's bloody hands and feet?

The Judgment of Paris

by Claude Lorrain (1600–1682)

Paris, a hero from Greek literature, was the son of the king of Troy. A vision warned that one day he would destroy the city of his birth, so his parents abandoned him on a mountainside. The child was saved and brought up by a shepherd. When Paris grew up, three goddesses

asked him to judge which of them was the most beautiful. Juno promised him land and riches if he chose her; Minerva offered victory in battle; and Aphrodite, the goddess of love, offered Paris the love of Helen, the most beautiful woman in the world. Paris, captivated by the description of Helen, picked Aphrodite.

With Aphrodite's help Paris met Helen in her home country, Greece. The couple fell in love and he stole her from her husband, who was the king, and took her back to Troy. But the episode caused a war between the Greeks and Trojans that ended in the destruction of Troy—the fatal prophecy had come true.

When Claude painted Paris judging the goddesses, he showed Juno, with her traditional companion the peacock, offering Paris great wealth. Minerva, with her spear and helmet, and Aphrodite, with her little son Cupid, wait to make their offers.

Although he was born in France, Claude fell in love with Italy, where he lived most of his life. Look how the figures only take up a small part of the picture while the rest is devoted to a peaceful Italian landscape. There is no hint of the terrible consequences that will follow Paris's decision.

The Nineteenth Century

As society changed dramatically, so did the role of art and artists. Artists were no longer required to paint religious images for churches. Increasingly they displayed their personal spiritual feelings in very original ways.

By the end of the 18th century the steam engine had been invented. The massive growth of industry that followed became known as the Industrial Revolution. As the numbers of factories, railroads, and steamboats grew throughout the 19th century, a new class of men and women appeared. With wealth gained from industry they soon became a very powerful group.

As the influence of the church and aristocracy weakened through the century, artists became increasingly reliant on selling their work to these new, wealthy clients. Such customers preferred to buy landscapes and portraits. Images of religious or mythological subjects fell out of favor.

A Romantic view

Despite the rise of materialism—with its emphasis on property and possessions rather than imagination or faith—many artists continued to look for inspiration in romances, the stories and ballads of the past. These painters became known as Romantics.

The Romantics believed that art should be a strong individual state-

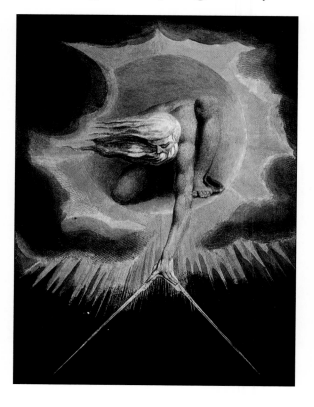

The Ancient of Days: William Blake
Blake was a very original painter and poet who created striking images from his vivid imagination and strong religious beliefs.

ment, expressing the artist's personal vision of the world, and feelings about it. There were no longer general beliefs that everyone held. For the first time there was a sense of distance, even conflict, between the artist and the public, which was to carry on into the 20th century.

A personal vision

One of the most visionary of all artists, William Blake, was a great inspiration to the Romantic movement. Although he was a deeply religious man, Blake's faith was individual and mystic. He did not produce work for the church. He wrote poems which he illustrated with drawings of his visions.

Look at the German artist Runge's painting of Mary and Joseph resting after their escape from King Herod.

It is a peaceful scene with a strange, haunting light. Like Blake's painting, this personal vision reflects a longing to return to a less materialistic age.

Other artists took aspects of faith as a subject they could portray. For example, Claude Monet's series of paintings of the cathedral in the French town of Rouen (*see page 29*) showed the changing effects of light on this enduring monument from a more spiritual past.

Rest on the Flight to Egypt:
Philipp Otto Runge
The wistful mood of Mary and Joseph is echoed in the subtle colors of the landscape.

Dido Building Carthage

by J.M.W. Turner (1775–1851)

When he was still a boy, the English painter Turner, it is said, looked at a painting by the 17th-century French artist Claude Lorrain (*see page 23*) and instantly burst into tears. When asked why he was crying, the young man replied that it was because he would never be able to paint a picture as good as the one in front of him. But years later, when Turner's painting based on the story of Dido, queen of the North African city of Carthage, went on show in London in 1815, many people said that his work was as good as Claude's.

In Roman myth Dido was the daughter of the king of Tyre in what is now Lebanon. Dido's brother Pygmalion murdered her husband to seize his treasure. Dido secretly fled from Tyre, together with a group of followers and much of her husband's wealth. When she arrived in North Africa, Dido asked the local inhabitants for some land. They said she could take as much as she could "enclose in the hide of a bull." This meant that she would only have a tiny bit of earth. But cunningly Dido cut the bull's hide into thin strips and tied them together to make a long cord. In this way she could surround a large plot of land. On this land she built the great city of Carthage.

In Turner's painting Dido is seen walking along the left bank of the river, inspecting her newly built city. But do you think telling the story is Turner's main interest? It is the sun that dominates the picture. Its light turns the sky orange and is reflected in the water below. In his fascination with sunlight Turner was inspired by Claude, said to be the first painter to capture a true impression of sunlight.

Rouen Cathedral

by Claude Monet (1840–1926)

In 1895 the French painter Monet told an interviewer that he was not interested in painting objects. He said he wanted instead to paint the atmosphere that lay behind them. The same year Monet exhibited a series of 20 paintings of the cathedral in the French town of Rouen, 18 of which were of the same part of the building. But each one was different. The pictures showed how the light at various times of the day altered what the cathedral looked like.

Monet was known as an Impressionist painter. His early pictures had

been "impressions"—painted in a single session with the subject of the painting in front of him. Monet had always been interested in the way that light altered how things looked. Increasingly, capturing these effects became more important to him than the subject itself.

By the time he began to paint Rouen Cathedral, Monet had developed a thorough and painstaking way of working. For several months in 1892 and again in 1893, he made studies of the cathedral. He set up his studio in a shop opposite and from this viewpoint kept a careful record of the way the sunlight changed the colors and shadows on the stone arches and turrets.

The many layers of paint on the finished canvases show how carefully Monet must have worked and reworked them. But just two years later, the artist was ready to exhibit all his paintings.

What time of day do you think this painting shows? Is it the bright light of morning or the more mellow, softer light of early evening? In fact, Monet painted it at noon, the hottest time of the day.

The Vision after the Sermon

by Paul Gauguin (1848–1903)

In the Bible story, when Jacob wanted to cross a river, his way was blocked by a man who would not let him pass. As Jacob struggled to get by, the man touched his thigh and it withered. Jacob began to wrestle with the man, and they fought all night. When day came at last, Jacob realized that his opponent was an angel, who blessed him for his bravery.

The French painter Gauguin shows Jacob and the angel in the middle of

their fight. A group of women, peasants wearing the traditional headresses of the remote French province of Brittany, are watching them. They have just left church, where the priest—on the right of the picture—has been telling them the biblical story. So strong is their belief in what they have heard that they "see" the fight taking place in the field in front of them. To heighten the difference between reality and the holy vision, Gauguin uses a tree to cut the picture in two and paints the field a deep red. This blood-red captures the intensity and drama of the story.

Gauguin was born in Paris and became a businessman, but moved to Brittany in 1886. He said the city did not inspire him to paint, and he wanted to live among people who led a simpler life. He even started to dress like a local fisherman, wearing a blue jersey and beret. Like Blake (*see page 24*), Gauguin had intensely strong religious feelings which he expressed in a personal, rather than a "realistic" way.

The Gates of Hell

by Auguste Rodin (1840–1917)

In earlier centuries artists such as Hieronymus Bosch had shown Hell as a land of fire and smoke (*see page 13*), where strange creatures tormented men and women who had sinned on Earth. But in the vision of Hell created by the French sculptor Rodin there are no terrifying devils or monstrous creatures. Instead there are 187 human figures.

In 1880 Rodin began to create a set of huge doors for a new museum.

Inspired by the Italian writer Dante's poem the *Inferno*—which described the different levels of suffering in Hell—Rodin set to work. But the museum was never built. And when Rodin died, 37 years later, he had not finished the bronze doors.

Rodin referred to the sculpture fondly as his "Noah's Ark." In the Bible story Noah collected the animals in the world to put in his ark, just as Rodin now put together many of his ideas for other sculptures in his work on the gates. Look at the man who sits above the doors, his head resting on his chin. This is a version of Rodin's sculpture *The Thinker*.

Rodin expresses pain and suffering through the poses of the bodies. The figures are taut and twisted. Some of them cling together, but many seem lonely and isolated; a few cling to the gates, while others seem about to fall. Rodin let his models move around the studio as he sketched them, to capture a sense of fluid movement. Look at the three figures at the top. Perhaps they remind you of the Three Graces (*see page 4*).

Rodin was not concerned that he had not completed this enormous project. A great work of art, he said, was never finished.

The Twentieth Century

Two world wars, economic depression, and other terrible events affected how people saw the world. Like many other people, artists questioned whether there was any room for either religion or myth in modern society.

As the 20th century began, many people were excited about the increasing speed of technological change. For the first time the world saw electric lighting, the telephone, the automobile, and the airplane. In this new age, some people said, there would no longer be any need for the myths and religions of the past.

One group of artists called themselves the Futurists to show their eagerness for the new technological age. In 1912 their leader Marinetti declared that a racing car was far more beautiful than the statues of ancient Greece. Not everyone agreed with him, however. Another group of artists, who became known as the Expressionists, tried to recapture some of the spiritual aspects of humanity which they believed had been lost in the new age. Like William Blake before him *(see page 24)*, the Expressionist painter Emil Nolde had a firm but personal Christian faith. His painting of the Last Supper is an attempt to reflect his own spirituality.

The Last Supper: Emil Nolde
The Expressionist artist Nolde ignored artistic tradition so that he could show his own feelings about the story of Christ.

In the shadow of war

The First World War of 1914 to 1918 brought a terrible number of deaths and casualties, more than any previous war. People's sense of optimism about the new century died, and many painters tried to reflect the inhumanity, chaos, and confusion of a world that could create suffering on such a scale.

There was more destruction to come in World War II during 1939 to 1945. Now lots of artists feared for the future. The twisted shapes and tortured faces in the images of the British painter Francis Bacon *(see page 43)* summed up the anxiety shared by many people during the second half of the century.

Many artists became interested in societies beyond Europe and the United States. At the turn of the century a collection of African masks went on display in France. This different kind of art, known as "primitive," inspired many artists.

Although the Englishman Henry Moore's sculpture is named "Madonna" for Mary, mother of Jesus, its style owes much to non-Christian cultures. Moore was fascinated by bold West African and Aztec images of their gods. He shows a Christian figure in a different way from the Western tradition.

Personal vision

Although artists continued to take inspiration from legends and myths of the ancient world, they no longer tried to tell the stories so people could recognize the characters and settings. Instead they began to use the subjects as starting points from which to explore their own ideas and feelings.

The French painter Odilon Redon *(see page 37)*, for example, used soft, merging colors to suggest a strange mythical story; Francis Bacon, meanwhile, portrayed a respected religious figure, a pope, in a terrifying way.

Madonna: Henry Moore
Look how huge and rounded these figures are. Like the Aztec art that Moore admired, this image is powerful in its simplicity.

Orpheus

by Odilon Redon (1840–1916)

When you look at this peaceful image, would you guess that it portrays the victim of a terrible, violent death? The body lies in a warm, golden landscape that has a calm, dreamlike feeling.

According to Greek legend, Orpheus was a musician of great skill. When he played the lyre—a stringed instrument a little like a harp—he charmed all the animals. Orpheus fell in love with a spirit of the woods

called Eurydice. One day, however, she was bitten by a snake and died. Orpheus missed her so much that he decided to go into the underworld, where the Greeks believed the spirits of the dead went, and bring her back.

Pluto, the king of the underworld, listened to the musician's pleas and agreed to return Eurydice to him on one condition. She would follow him back to the surface, but he must not look back or she would be lost forever. Orpheus agreed and set off. But he could not resist one glance back to check that Eurydice really was there.

As he had threatened, Pluto took Eurydice away for ever. The grief-stricken Orpheus grew to hate all women. Finally he was torn apart by a group of women who worshipped the wine god, Bacchus.

In Redon's painting the head of the dead Orpheus, the eyes closed, floats above the strings of his lyre. Above him strange flowers sprout from the foothills of a mountain. Redon does not show a particular moment from the story but instead tries to evoke a mood with color and simple images. Why do you think Redon made his image so peaceful? Perhaps it is to suggest the end of Orpheus's suffering and the beauty of his music.

White Crucifixion

by Marc Chagall (1887–1985)

In 1917 revolution swept through Russia. The violent event sent shock waves around the world. The new Russian government was communist and it made profound changes in the country; it even outlawed all religions.

Many Russians left the country. Among them was the painter Marc Chagall, who was born into a Russian Jewish family. He left his homeland and settled in France, but the memory of the harsh treatment of the Jews in Russia remained with him. Not only that, the Jews also began to suffer from violent prejudice elsewhere in Europe, particularly in Germany. When Chagall painted his version of the Crucifixion of Jesus in 1938, he reflected his anxieties about these anti-Jewish feelings.

Look back at Grünewald's picture of the Crucifixion (*see page 15*). There the artist focuses your attention on Christ himself. But in this picture Chagall has made Jesus a symbol of the suffering of the Jewish people. Jesus wears a Jewish prayer shawl, and above his head is an inscription in the ancient Jewish language of Hebrew that reads "Jesus of Nazareth, King of the Jews." Above him float figures from the Old Testament.

Look at all the action around Jesus: it reflects real events that happened during the artist's lifetime. A group of soldiers waving the red flag of the Communists sets fire to a village. Meanwhile, to the right, a group of German Nazis attack a Jewish temple, or synagogue. Images of war, chaos, and panic fill the canvas.

Although this painting has a violent subject, it is painted in a simple way. Despite his exile, Chagall never forgot the folk painting of his native country, and this is reflected in his style.

Pasiphaë

by Jackson Pollock (1912–1956)

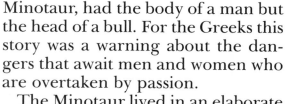

Look hard at this painting. Can you see any shapes you recognize among the splashes of paint? Perhaps the artist did not intend you to be able to see particular things but wanted to suggest feelings and emotions. Does the painting seem lively or calm? Happy or sad?

Pasiphaë appears in one of the strangest of all the ancient Greek legends. She was the wife of the king of the Mediterranean island of Crete. Pasiphaë fell in love with a bull and gave birth to a frightening creature. This grotesque monster, known as the Minotaur, had the body of a man but the head of a bull. For the Greeks this story was a warning about the dangers that await men and women who are overtaken by passion.

The Minotaur lived in an elaborate maze beneath its mother's palace, eating young men and women who were sacrificed to it. Finally the hero Theseus killed it. Pasiphaë's daughter Ariadne gave him a ball of thread to unravel as he entered the maze so that he could find his way out again.

Does knowing the story make you look at this picture in a different way?

Originally the American painter Jackson Pollock called the painting *Moby Dick* after the great whale in Herman Melville's famous novel. But as he worked on the picture, Pollock decided to name it after the Greek myth. Perhaps he decided that the title was not really important.

Pollock was attracted to this story because it allowed him to explore exciting and violent emotions. Among the swirls of color are suggestions of limbs and heads. He tried to capture a sense of drama and intensity rather than attempting to tell Pasiphaë's story in detail.

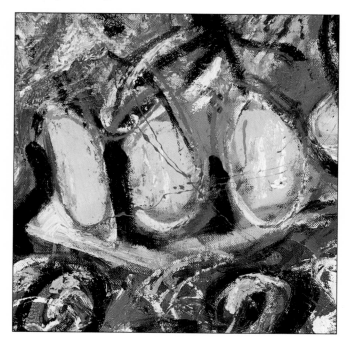

Pope Innocent X

by Francis Bacon (1909–1992)

This picture is based on a 300-year-old portrait. In 1650 the Spanish painter Velázquez was asked to paint one of the most powerful men in the world—the head of the Catholic Church, Pope Innocent X. At the time there were strict rules governing the portrayal of powerful men. Velázquez painted a lifelike but respectful portrait of the churchman.

In the hands of the British painter Francis Bacon, however, the dignified

figure has become the center of a nightmare vision. The pope's mouth is open as though in a silent scream; he clutches the arms of his chair as if he were terrified. Black emptiness surrounds him, and great smears of paint give the impression that he is sitting in a cage. Red paint is splattered like blood across the canvas.

Notice the restless sense of energy that Bacon has given his figure. Velázquez's pope was very still and calm, as though to suggest the unchanging power of the Church. Perhaps Bacon's image suggests that the Church has changed; more people today question the teachings of the Bible.

Bacon was fascinated by certain images that he painted again and again. He found illustrations of diseases of the mouth in a medical textbook. Bacon used an open mouth in many pictures; although he said it was not meant to suggest any particular emotion, here it seems as though the pope is screaming in agony.

Another image Bacon often used in his paintings was from an early Russian movie, showing a woman in round glasses screaming. Bacon gives the pope the same glasses but leaves his eyes blank, emphasizing the terrible look on his face.

GLOSSARY

abstract art: art that does not represent objects or people that can be recognized in the real world, but which expresses a thought, idea, or feeling through colors and shapes.

Baroque: a 17th and 18th century art movement that used elaborate and theatrical forms to appeal to the viewer's emotions.

classical art: the painting and sculpture of ancient Greece and Rome.

Cubism: a 20th-century painting style that showed the structure of things, often by displaying different views of the subject at the same time.

Expressionism: a style of art in which color and form are used to suggest moods and feelings rather than mimic what is seen.

fresco: a way of painting on walls in which color is applied straight onto a layer of wet plaster.

Futurism: an art movement that used new techniques to express the excitement and dynamism of the early 20th century.

Impressionism: a style of painting in which artists tried to capture the effects of light and the atmosphere of a scene.

Industrial Revolution: a period of rapid technological change in the early 19th century when many Western countries were transformed by new machines and industries.

medium: the material with which a work of art is created, such as pencil, oil, or watercolor.

Middle Ages: the period of European history that lasted from about the fifth to the 15th centuries.

naïve art: a name given to art produced by untrained artists who often do not use advanced techniques such as perspective.

naturalism: an approach to art in which everyday objects, places, and people are shown without trying to idealize their appearance.

oil paint: a type of paint that uses oils to bind together the color.

pastel: crayons made from chalk and powdered pigment, which smudge on paper.

perspective: a method of drawing used to create an illusion of depth in a flat picture, using lines that meet at a single spot on the horizon known as the "vanishing point."

portrait: a painting that gives a likeness of a person and often an insight into his or her personality.

primitivism: a type of art that uses the shapes and symbols of tribal cultures from, for example, Africa, South America, or Asia.

realism: an approach to art that sees even ugly and unhappy scenes as being suitable subjects for artists.

Reformation: a 16th-century religious movement that protested many of the ideas of the Catholic Church and established the Protestant faith.

Renaissance: the "rebirth" of classical ideas that began in 14th century Italy, lasted to the 17th century, and led to a flowering of the visual arts and literature.

Rococo: An art movement of the early 18th century that used a delicate, elegant, decorative style.

Romanticism: a 19th-century movement in art and literature that celebrated the exotic, passionate, and dangerous.

sketch: a rough or quick version of a picture, often produced as a trial-run for a more finished work.

still life: a drawing or painting of objects that cannot move by themselves, such as fruit and flowers.

Surrealism: a 20th-century art movement that combines odd images to express the irrational and subconscious world of dreams or fantasy.

technique: the way an artist uses his or her materials.

watercolor: a type of paint in which colors dissolve in water.

looking at art
SET INDEX

Page numbers in italic refer to subjects with illustrations; numbers in bold are volume numbers

abstract art **1:** 34; **2:** 35; **7:** 40, 42; **8:** 38; **9:** 36-37, 42; **11:** 37; **12:** 34
African masks **1:** *35*; **6:** 35
Ahearn, John **5:** *33*
America, *see* United States of America
Anderson, Sophie **5:** *24*
Armstrong, Louis **4:** *33*

Bacon, Francis **6:** 35, *42*
Balla, Giacomo **10:** 37, *42*
Baroque art **6:** 16
Bellini, Giovanni **9:** *12*; **12:** 6
Bellows, George **4:** *36*
Benton, Thomas Hart **4:** 33, *38*
Bernini, Gianlorenzo **6:** *16*
Bible stories **1:** *6, 12*; **2:** 32; **3:** *6, 8,* 10, *16*; **4:** *8*; **6:** 4, 5, 8, *10, 14, 17, 20, 25, 30, 32, 34*; **8:** 6, 16; **9:** *5, 14, 20*; **10:** 14, 18, 26; **11:** *4, 5, 6,* 10, *12,* 24; **12:** *6, 12, 16*
Bingham, George Caleb **11:** *26*
Blake, William **6:** *24*; **7:** 30, 34
Boccioni, Umberto **7:** *34*
Bonnard, Pierre **3:** 34, *40*
Bosch, Hieronymus **1:** *12*; **6:** *12*

Botticelli, Sandro **6:** *5*; **11:** *8*
Boucher, François **3:** *18*; **11:** *20*
Braque, Georges **8:** 34, 35, *38*
Britain **2:** 36; **3:** 15; **4:** 20, 24; **7:** 24; **9:** 28; **10:** 16, 25, 32; **11:** 28
Bronzino, Agnolo **5:** *12*; **11:** *10*
Brown, Ford Madox **2:** *28*
Brueghel the Elder, Jan **8:** 5, *12*, 28
Brueghel the Elder, Pieter **2:** *10*; **4:** 5, *12*; **5:** *10*; **7:** *12*; **9:** *16*; **12:** 5, *10*
Burra, Edward **1:** *42*; **7:** *33*

Campin, Robert **2:** *8*; **3:** *8*
Canaletto (Giovanni Antonio Canal) **7:** 16, *22*; **11:** *15*
Carracci, Annibale **2:** *12*; **8:** *5*
Caravaggio, Michelangelo Merisi da **6:** *18*, 20; **8:** *16*; **10:** *18*
Cassatt, Mary **3:** *30*; **5:** *28*
Catholic Church **2:** 5, 14; **4:** 14; **6:** 4, 16, 42; **7:** 14; **8:** 4; **11:** 4
cave painting **10:** 6
Cézanne, Paul **4:** *31*; **8:** 25, *32*; **9:** 34
Chagall, Marc **6:** *38*
Chardin, Jean Baptiste **8:** *14*
China **7:** 8; **9:** *6*; **11:** 15
Christ **1:** 4, *6, 12*; **2:** *8*; **3:** 4, 6, 8, *16*; **4:** 5, *8*; **5:** *4*, 5, *8*;

6: *10, 14, 20, 38*; **9:** 12, *14*; **11:** *6*; **12:** *6, 12*
Claesz, Pieter **8:** *15*
classical civilization **1:** 4; **3:** 4; **4:** 4-5; **5:** 5; **6:** 4, 5, 6; **7:** 4, 18; **10:** 4
Claude Lorrain **6:** *22*, 26; **9:** *20*; **12:** 14, *16*
Constable, John **9:** *28*; **12:** *26*
Copley, John Singleton **12:** 15, *18*
Courbet, Gustave **2:** 24-25, *26*; **8:** *24*
Cranach, Lucas **9:** *14*; **10:** *14*
Crete **10:** *8*; **12:** 8
Cubism **8:** 34

Dadaism 1: 40
Dali, Salvador **8:** 35, *40*
David, Jacques-Louis **1:** *20*; **3:** *24*
de Hooch, *see* Hooch, Pieter de
Degas, Edgar **1:** *22*; **2:** *30*; **3:** 30; **5:** 25, 28; **10:** 25, *30*
Delacroix, Eugène **8:** *26*; **10:** 24, *28*; **12:** 36
Derain, André **9:** *40*
Disney, Walt **10:** 37
Duchamp, Marcel **1:** 35, *40*
Dürer, Albrecht **8:** 5, *8*; **10:** *5*
Dyck, *see* van Dyck

Egyptian art **2:** 6
El Greco **7:** *14*
England, *see* Britain
Etruscan art **4:** 4
Exekias **4:** *5*

Expressionism **1:** 34; **6:** 34; **10:** 38; **11:** 36, 38; **12:** 40
Eyck, *see* van Eyck

Fauvism 9: 40
Fragonard, Jean-Honoré **4:** *15;* **9:** *24*
France **2:** 32; **3:** 15, 22, 24; **4:** 30; **5:** 36; **9:** 24, 27, 34; **10:** 6
French Revolution **1:** 20; **3:** 15, 22, 24; **9:** 24, 26
fresco **3:** 4, 6, 8; **6:** 8; **9:** 8; **11:** 4, *see also* wall painting
Freud, Sigmund **1:** 34; **5:** 32; **9:** 36
Friedrich, Caspar David **9:** *26;* **12:** *20*
Futurism **6:** 34; **7:** 32-33, 34; **10:** 42; **11:** 36, 38

Gainsborough, Thomas **5:** *22;* **9:** *22*
Gauguin, Paul **1:** *23,* 34; **2:** *25;* **8:** 28; **6:** *30;* **10:** *34*
genre painting **2:** 14; **3:** 14; **7:** 20
Gentileschi, Artemesia **6:** *17*
Géricault, Théodore **12:** *22*
Germany **1:** 38; **3:** 36; **4:** 42; **8:** 8; **9:** 14, 42; **12:** 40
Ghirlandaio, Domenico **3:** *5*
Giorgione **12:** *5*
Giotto **1:** *6;* **3:** *6;* **5:** *4,* 5, 8
Gogh, *see* van Gogh
Goncharova, Natalia **2:** *40*
Goya, Francisco de **10:** *25*
Gozzoli, Benozzo **9:** *6*
Grosz, George **1:** 35, *38;* **4:** *42;* **7:** 33, *36*
Grünewald, Matthias **6:** *14*

Hals, Frans **1:** *15;* **5:** *14*
Harnett, William **8:** *30*
Hicks, Edward **10:** *25,* 26

Hine, Lewis **2:** *34;* **3:** *34;* **5:** *38*
Hiroshige, Ando **12:** 21, *24*
Hockney, David **3:** *42;* **11:** *42*
Hogarth, William **3:** *14, 15;* **4:** 14, *18;* **5:** *20;* **7:** *17*
Hokusai, Katsushika **12:** *21*
Holbein the Younger, Hans **1:** *5;* **3:** *12;* **8:** *10*
Holland, *see* Netherlands
Homer, Winslow **12:** *32*
Hooch, Pieter de **3:** *20;* **7:** 16, *20*
Hopper, Edward **2:** *42;* **4:** 33, *40*

Impressionism 1: 22-23; **3:** 23, 30, 40; **4:** 23; **5:** 26, 28**; 6:** 28; **7:** 25, 28, 30; **9:** 27, 32, 34; **10:** 24, 30; **11:** 26–27, 34
Industrial Revolution **2:** 24; **3:** 22; **6:** 24; **7:** 38; **11:** 26
Ingres, Jean-Auguste-Dominique **1:** *24*
Italy **2:** 12; **3:** 4, 6; **4:** 8; **7:** 5, 16; **9:** 4, 19; **10:** 4, 12; **11:** 4

Japan 4: 16; **11:** 15, 16; **12:** 21, 24
Jesus, *see* Christ
Johnson, Eastman **3:** *26*

Kahlo, Frida **5:** *42*
Kandinsky, Wassily **3:** 36; **9:** 36, *42;* **12:** 35, *38*
Kauffmann, Angelica **2:** *14*
Klimt, Gustav **9:** *37*
Kokoschka, Oskar **5:** *40*
Kyuhaku, Kano Naganobu **4:** *16*

Landseer, Edwin **10:** *32*

Lange, Dorothea **3:** *35*
Leonardo da Vinci **1:** *40;* **6:** *10;* **11:** *5*
Lichtenstein, Roy **12:** 35
Limbourg brothers **2:** *5;* **4:** *6;* **7:** *10*
Lorrain, *see* Claude Lorrain
Lorenzetti, Ambrogio **9:** *8*
Lowry, L.S. **7:** *38*

Magritte, René **12:** *42*
Manet, Édouard **1:** 23, *26;* **3:** *28;* **8:** *25*
Mannerism **7:** 14
Mantegna, Andrea **10:** *12;* **12:** *4*
Marc, Franz **10:** *38;* **11:** 36, *38*
Marin, John **11:** *37*
Masaccio **5:** *8;* **6:** *8*
"Master of Moulins" **5:** *6*
Massys, Quentin **8:** *6*
Mexican artists **5:** *42;* **2:** *38*
Michelangelo **2:** *4*
Middle Ages **1:** 5; **2:** 5; **4:** 5; **8:** 4; **6:** 4, 5; **12:** 5
Millais, John Everett **11:** *30*
Minotaur **6:** *40;* **10:** 8
Modigliani, Amedeo **1:** 34, *36*
Mondrian, Piet **7:** 33, *40;* **11:** *40*
Monet, Claude **6:** 25, *28;* **7:** *28;* **9:** 27, *32;* **11:** 27, *34*
Moore, Henry **6:** 35
Morisot, Berthe **5:** *26*
Munch, Edvard **9:** *38*
Münter, Gabriel **3:** 34, *36*
mural, *see* wall painting
mythology **1:** 18; **6:** 4, 5, 6, 18, 22, 36, 40; **9:** 16; **11:** 8; **12:** 8

naïve art **4:** 33, 34; **10:** 24, 26
Netherlands **1:** 16; **2:** 8, 14;

3: 14; **4:** 12, 14; **5:** 14; **9:** 10, 18; **11:** 14, 18, 40; **12:** 5, 10, 14

New York **3:** 24, 38; **4:** 36, 38, 40; **7:** 24, 33, 40, 42

Nolde, Emil **6:** *34*; **12:** 35, *40*

O'Keeffe, Georgia **7:** *42*; **10:** *40*

perspective 2: 40; **3:** 4, 8; **5:** 8; **6:** 5; **7:** 5; **9:** 4, 5; **11:** 4, 5

photography **1:** 23; **2:** 24, 30, 34, 35, 36; **3:** 35; **4:** 33; **7:** 24; **8:** 34; **9:** 36, 37; **11:** 36; **12:** 35

Picasso, Pablo **1:** 34, *35*; **5:** *36*; **8:** *35*; **10:** *36*

Piero della Francesca **1:** *10*; **4:** *8*; **7:** *5-6*; **11:** *6*

pointillism **11:** 32

Pollock, Jackson **6:** *40*

Pop art **8:** 42; **12:** 34

Poussin, Nicolas **4:** *14*; **7:** *18*; **11:** *24*

Pre-Raphaelites **11:** 26

Protestantism **1:** 14; **2:** 5, 14; **3:** 5, 14; **4:** 14; **7:** 16, 20; **6:** 16; **9:** 18; **11:** 14

Redon, Odilon **5:** *34*; **6:** *36*; **8:** 34, *36*

Rembrandt van Rijn **1:** 14, *16*; **2:** *18*; **8:** *18*; **10:** *20*; **11:** *22*

Renaissance **1:** 5; **2:** 5, 38; **3:** 4; **4:** 10, 14; **5:** 5; **6:** 4, 5; **7:** 5; **9:** 4; **10:** 4; **11:** 4-5

Renoir, Pierre-Auguste **7:** 25, *30*

Reynolds, Joshua **1:** 14-15, *18*

Rivera, Diego **2:** *38*

Rococo **3:** 15, 18

Rodin, Auguste **6:** *32*

Roman art **1:** *4*; **6:** 4; **7:** *6*; **8:** *4*; **9:** *4*; **10:** *4*

Romanticism **6:** 24-25; **9:** 26; **10:** 24, 28; **12:** 20-21

Rousseau, Henri **4:** 33, *34*; **12:** *36*

Rubens, Peter Paul **5:** *16*, 18; **6:** *20*; **9:** 19; **10:** 22, 28

Ruisdael, Jacob van **9:** *18*; **11:** *14*; **12:** 15

Runge, Philipp Otto **6:** 25

Russia **2:** 40; **6:** 38; **12:** 38

Ruysch, Rachel **8:** *20*

Sargent, John Singer **4:** *26*; **5:** *30*

sculpture **1:** *4*; **2:** *4*; **5:** *5*, 25; **6:** *4*, 6, *32*; **8:** *35*; **10:** *4*, *8*, 12, *36*; **11:** 6

Seurat, Georges **4:** *22*; **11:** *32*

Sharaku, Toshusai **1:** *28*

Sloan, John **2:** 35

Sotatsu, Tawaraya **11:** *16*

Spain **2:** 16; **4:** 26; **5:** 36; **7:** 14; **8:** 22; **10:** 24

Spencer, Stanley **2:** 35, 36

Stubbs, George **2:** *15*; **10:** *17*

Surrealism **12:** 42

Talbot, William Henry Fox **7:** *25*

Tiepolo, Giambattista **12:** *14*

Tintoretto (Jacopo Robusti) **11:** *12*; **12:** 5, *12*

Tissot, James **4:** *24*

Titian **4:** *10*; **12:** 5, *8*

Toulouse-Lautrec, Henri de **1:** *32*; **4:** *22*

Turner, J.M.W. **6:** *26*; **7:** 25, 26; **9:** *30*; **11:** *28*; **12:** *28*

Uccello, Paolo **11:** *4*; **10:** *10*

United States **1:** 42; **2:** 35; **3:** 15, 22, 26, 30, 34, 35,

38; **4:** 20, 33, 38, 40, 42; **5:** 28; **7:** 24, 25; **10:** 25, 26, 40; **11:** 26

U.S. artists **2:** *34*, *35*, *42*; **3:** *26*, *30*, *32*, *34*, *35*, *38*; **4:** *26*, *36*, *38*, *40*; **5:** 28, *30*, *33*, *38*; **6:** *40*; **7:** *42*; **8:** *30*, *42*; **10:** *26*, *40*; **11:** 36, *37*; **12:** *32*, 34, *35*

van Dyck, Anthony **5:** *15*, 22

van Eyck, Jan **1:** 5, *8*; **3:** *10*; **9:** *10*

van Gogh, Vincent **1:** *30*; **2:** 24, 25, *32*; **3:** *23*; **4:** 23, 28; **8:** *28*; **9:** *27*; **11:** *27*; **12:** *30*

van Ruisdael, *see* Ruisdael

Velázquez, Diego **2:** *16*; **3:** *16*; **5:** *18*; **6:** *6*

Venus de Milo **6:** *6*

Vermeer, Jan **2:** *20*; **11:** *18*

Verrocchio, Andrea del **5:** *5*

wall painting **2:** 6, 38; **4:** 38; **5:** 4; **6:** 10; **7:** 6; **8:** 4; **9:** 4, **10:** 12; **11:** 10, *see also* fresco

Warhol, Andy **8:** 35, *42*

Whistler, James Abbott McNeill **3:** *32*

Wood, Grant **3:** 38

World War I **1:** 35, 38; **5:** 30; **6:** 34; **7:** 36; **9:** 36; **11:** 38

World War II **2:** 35, 36, 38; **4:** 40, 42; **6:** 34

Wright of Derby, Joseph **2:** *22*; **4:** 20

Zhang Zeduan **7:8**

Zola, Emile **3:** 28

Zurbarán, Francisco **8:** *22*

FURTHER READING

Cummings, Pat, ed. *Talking with Artists*. Bradbury, 1992.

Greenberg, Jan, and Jordan, Sandra. *The Painter's Eye: Learning to Look at Contemporary Art*. Delacorte, 1991.

Isaacson, Philip M. *A Short Walk Around the Pyramids & Through the World of Art*. Knopf, 1993.

Janson, H.W. *History of Art*. Harry N. Abrams, Inc., 1995.

Powell, Jillian. *Painting and Sculpture*. Steck-Vaughn, 1990.

Sills, Leslie. *Visions: Stories about Women Artists*. Albert Whitman, 1993.

Testa, Fulvio. *If You Take a Paintbrush: A Book of Colors*. Dial, 1983.

Waterford, Giles. *Faces*. Atheneum, 1982.

Woolf, Felicity. *Picture This: A First Introduction to Paintings*. Doubleday, 1990

Yenawine, Philip. *Colors*. Delacorte, 1991; *Lines*. Delacorte, 1991; *Shapes*. Delacorte, 1991.

Zadrzynska, Ewa. *The Girl with a Watering Can*. Chameleon, 1990.